BEYOND THE FRAME

GREAT RACING PHOTOGRAPHS

EDWARD WHITAKER

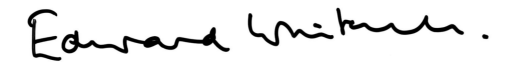

RACING POST

To my parents James and Iwona

This edition first published in Great Britain in 2011 by
Racing Post Books, Compton, Newbury, Berkshire, RG20 6NL

10 9 8 7 6 5 4 3 2 1

A catalogue record for this book is available from the
British Library

ISBN 978-1-905156-85-6

Designed by Soapbox
www.soapbox.co.uk

Printed in the UK by Butler, Tanner and Dennis, Frome

www.racingpost.com/shop

CONTENTS

WILDFLOWER JILLY

Jilly Cooper next to her home near Stroud
in September 2010. Jilly revels in nature and
I thought she looked great in this setting. We
went down to see some ponies but the paddock
was full of these wildflowers so I asked her to
walk through them.

FOREWORD

If genius is the infinitive capacity for taking pains, this sums up Edward Whitaker. Summer, Winter, night or day, at home or abroad, you will find him at the races: watching, lurking, sweating up as much as any of his equine subjects, as he hurtles down course and across parade ring, or lies, scattered with brushwood beneath vast fences, to catch the perfect shot.

The racehorse is one of the fastest things on the planet. Edward's secret is the speed with which, kissing the joy as it flies, he captures this poetry in motion.

Uniquely privileged to be one of his subjects, as you can see, I have experienced this speed. Other great photographers have spent up to five hours on a sitting. Edward took five minutes, whisking me across the valley into a clump of Himalayan Balsam, then snap! snap! Perfection.

In this most beautiful collection of photographs, you will find racing's entire cast: owners, trainers, jockeys united in camaraderie and rivalry, stable lads, farriers, bookies, punters, star-struck celebrities, not to mention top-hatted toffs ogling women as beautifully sleek and glossy mane-tossing as any of the horses.

You will meet the major players, imperious hawk-like Sheiks, Sir Henry Cecil, long fingers joined in prayer to thank a winning horse, a mellow J.P. enjoying Christmas with his terriers and ginger cat.

Nor will you be in any doubt that photography is an art form – as you marvel over horses floodlit against an indigo Dubai sky, or, with steam from their nostrils mingling with the morning mist, in landscapes to rival any Gainsborough or Stubbs.

It is also the variety of Edward's work that enchants, how it ranges from the agony of a Queen losing a Derby, to the white hot ecstasy of A.P. McCoy at last nailing the National. Most touching are the close-up photo-finishes, showing the courage of eyeballing, flattened-eared horses frantically striving to get their noses in front. Each picture tells a story – please let the lonely little chestnut in a vast sales ring go to a congenial home.

Finally, there is the wizardry and wit of Whitaker, the eye for detail that shows Frankie Dettori flying from a winning horse in front of a row of 'Fly Emirates' posters or the impeccable colour sense which juxtaposes a semi-circle of scarlet geraniums with the red livery of the Queen's outriders.

Everyone in racing is familiar with Edward's photographs but this stunning collection should appeal to a far wider public and I hope will bring this public flooding to the races to fall in love with our glorious sport.

Jilly Cooper
Gloucestershire
2011

The Kit

In my camera bag I have a notepad and pencil
and two Nikon D3 bodies.

As for lenses I have:
500mm/F4
300mm/F2.8
70–200mm/F2.8
24–70mm/F2.8
14–24mm/F2.8
10.5mm/F2.8

Accessories:
1.4 x and 1.7 x converters
SB 800 flash
Pocket Wizards (for firing remote camera)

Clothing:
Fleeces (layers are the trick)
EMS Waterproofs for all weathers bought in New York
Aigle Wellingtons
Gortex Timberland Boots
Fingerless gloves
Skiing Hat
Thermal Socks
Mobile Phone

THE WINNING PORTFOLIO

Sports Journalists Association Sports Photographer of the Year 2008

To win this award and to be presented with the Ed Lacey Trophy by Dame Kelly Holmes was the most memorable moment of my career so far.

To follow past recipients such as my mentors, Chris Smith, Bob Martin and David Ashdown gave me huge satisfaction, especially as I had only one subject – horseracing – rather than the more usual ten different sports.

The important thing with portfolios is to present ten different aspects of a sport. Equally, the impact of the image can be enormously improved by the way the picture is cropped.

For example, the shot of Frankie Dettori celebrating at the Breeders' Cup (see page 16) was tremendously improved by actually eliminating the horse's head, thereby putting all the focus on the jubilant jockey himself.

Yet the most satisfying aspect for me was to have my photography recognised by such a distinguished group of judges. You don't start off each year trying to build a portfolio but as 2008 developed I began to think I had a number of strong images with which to work. Let me take you through to the end result. This is how it all came together.

I. THE PRANCING HORSE

2. FOUR WAY FINISH

3. MOON OVER GREAT LEIGHS

4. 24 HOURS IN THE WEST, TENBY BEACH

5. STEAMING HORSE

6. AUTUMN LIGHT

7. 24 HOURS IN PASADENA, BACK FROM THE TRACK

8. FULL STRETCH

9. L. DETTORI IN EXCELCIS

IO. THREE FACES ON A WALL

PORTFOLIO PHOTOS

1. THE PRANCING HORSE

Teofilio feels his oats at Newmarket,
10 July 2008.

Each July there is a parade of Sheikh
Mohammed's Darley stallions at Dalham Hall
Stud in Newmarket. Wanting to get a stallion
in the more natural environment of a field rather
than a parade ring, I asked Sam Farrell the
stallion man if he would take Teofilio outside.
Almost immediately he reared up to give this
ultimate symbol of manhood. No wonder
Ferrari have it on their cars.

Nikon D2X, ISO 100, 1/640 at f/5.6

2. FOUR WAY FINISH

Nassau Stakes at Goodwood, 2 August 2008.

That was one of those finishes to dream about.
Four fillies locked together at the end of a
Group One race on a sunny day at Glorious
Day Goodwood. The Johnny Murtagh ridden
winner even had the perfect name – Halfway
to Heaven.

Nikon D2X, ISO 250, 1/2500 at f/4.8

3. MOON OVER GREAT LEIGHS

Horses at the ill-fated Great Leighs,
19 September 2008.

Great Leighs may have 'gone under' within
a year but it provided me with wonderful
pictures. The forecast for this day was that
there would be a dramatic sunset. This did
not happen. Later, however, a huge Harvest
Moon rose quickly over the stalls for the
One mile start and, by coincidence, had the
same brightness as that of the floodlights
illuminating the horses on the track.

Nikon D2X, ISO 800, 1/200 at f/2.8

4. 24 HOURS IN THE WEST

Hills of Aran, ridden by trainer's wife,
Linda Goldsworthy, South Beach, Tenby,
8 October 2008.

Sometimes everything comes together, no
matter what problems are encountered on
the way. Welsh trainer Keith Goldsworthy
had a good hurdler, Hills of Aran. He invited
me to go to Tenby, adding 'It's much more
spectacular than Deauville.' A week later I
drove from Newmarket to Pembrokeshire to
get the promised photo. It was one of those
cloudy, drizzly – but bright days. The tide was
out. Everything worked out – it's just a lovely,
peaceful picture.

Nikon D2X, ISO 100, 1/640 at f/6.3

5. STEAMING HORSE

Trainer Evan Williams and Golden Feather
at Llancarfan, 9 October 2008.

From Tenby I headed East to the Vale of
Glamorgan and spent the next morning
shooting a feature on rugby loving Evan
Williams. The sun was beginning to come
through the mist and the big dip in the lane
by his yard meant that you could shoot into
deep shadows which were lit from behind by
this golden glow. What really makes the picture
is the direction of the steam which perfectly
emphasises the profiles of horse and man.

Nikon D2X, ISO 100, 1/640 at f/5.6

6. AUTUMN LIGHT

Poplars at Newbury.

October is a great month for photographs.
As I drove home down the M4 it was such
a gorgeous afternoon that I dropped off at
Newbury races to see if I could find a picture.
Towards the end of the card there was a long
distance race that would actually go past these
poplars which were being lit by the dipping sun.
So I shot from the press room balcony and as
the horses went past they helped make this
classic Autumnal scene.

Nikon D2X, ISO 100, 1/320 at f/4.5

7. 24 HOURS IN PASADENA
BACK FROM THE TRACK

Dawn at Santa Anita – Breeders Cup Morning,
24 October 2008.

In October the sun does not rise in California
until 7 am even if the sky is clear. So by the time
I shot this picture the group of horses and riders
– in silhouette – had already done their work.
Look at the elbow of the rider closest to the sun.
Only after the gallops, not before, would it be
as relaxed as this.

Nikon D3, ISO 200, 1/500 at f/11

8. FULL STRETCH

Ballyfitz and Paddy Brennan at Cheltenham,
15 November 2008.

On this day the third last at Cheltenham
offered drama, sunlight and – increasingly
rare nowadays – no advertising. When horses
overjump, as Ballyfitz has, it makes the image
much more exciting. Note the reins at the
buckle end and Brennan's lower leg completely
extended. Better still the arc of his jump has
made a perfect frame for the runner up Big Fella
Thanks on whom Ruby Walsh is completing
a contrastingly orthodox leap.

Nikon D2X, ISO 200, 1/2500 at f/4

9. L. DETTORI IN EXCELCIS

Donatavium wins the Breeders' Cup Juvenile
Turf, 25 October 2008.

'Lanfranco' always makes great pictures. He
is the most charismatic and photogenic racing
character in the world. There is no one like
him and with two Breeders' Cup winners this
was the sort of big day Frankie saves himself
for. This is not the showmanship celebration
that comes later, this was the absolute winning
post moment of delight.

Nikon D3, ISO 200, 1/800 at f/5.6

10. THREE FACES ON A WALL

Betting Windows at Santa Anita – Day 2
Breeders' Cup, 25 October 2008.

Quirkiness can make great photographs.
These three looked like characters from that
poster for *The Usual Suspects*. What really makes
it is the different sizes of the three people and
the deadpan way they are eyeing me up.

Nikon D3, ISO 1600, 1/250 at f/2.8

THE WHITAKER COLLECTION

Following the first collection of photographs in my book, *In The Frame*, I wanted this second collection to highlight the moods and personalities of the diverse characters who populate the wonderful world of horseracing.

As you turn the pages you will find the emotions of celebration and success, the misery of failure, the stunning landscapes of the racetracks and gallops and the myriad personalities who contribute into our noble sport.

I hope you enjoy the pictures as much as I enjoyed taking them.

STONEHENGE BETTING RING

The sun sets on the betting ring at Folkestone racecourse in January 2008. Silhouettes can create graphic images and here are these monolithic figures rising out of the ground.

📷 Nikon D2X, ISO 100, 1/500 at f/9

Johnny Murtagh reaches for the sky in June 2008 as he brings Yeats in for the third of the horse's record four Ascot Gold Cup victories. There was both power and prayer in this moment. You could feel it.

Nikon D2X, ISO 100, 1/640 at f/5.6

Stanley House Stud, 2008. Classic and Breeders'
Cup winner Ouija Board canters with her first
foal, a colt by Kingmambo (later to be called
Voodoo Prince). As they came past, the pair
were in perfect unison.

Nikon D2X, ISO 100, 1/500 at f/4.5

STUDY IN SCARLET

Some people say colour does not matter but just look at this. It won Charlotte Weber the 'Best Dressed Lady' prize at Newmarket in July 2008.

📷 Nikon D2X, ISO 100, 1/500 at f/4.5

HAYLEY'S SMILE

The great thing about the Ascot weighing room
is that the light diffuses through the opaque
roof. It gives the perfect light for portraits –
even spontaneous ones like this.

📷 Nikon D2X, ISO 100, 1/500 at f/4.5

Stable jockey Mick Kinane wears Ballydoyle's singular dark blue Magnier silks alongside his three stablemates in the paddock before the 2007 St Leger at Doncaster. He looks happy but he got beat a length by the John Gosden-trained Lucarno.

📷 Nikon D2X, ISO 200, 1/500 at f/5.6

DUBAI MODELS AT 'THE DESERT PARTY
EXTRAVAGANZA'

To announce Sheikh Mohammed's extraordinary
racecourse Meydan. Naturally, beautiful girls are
attracted to such events. They were not in short
supply on this evening.

📷 Nikon D2X, ISO 250, 1/2 at f/2.8

FRANKIE SALUTES AMERICA

Raven's Pass has just won the 2009 Breeders' Cup Classic at Santa Anita. It was Frankie's greatest ever success in America and he was plucking the flowers from the garland and tossing them in the air. It was as if he was sprinkling stardust for my picture.

📷 Nikon D3, ISO 200,1/640 at f/6.3

THE GREEN EYE

It hurts if you don't make the finals. An ignored
contender wonders why on Ladies Day at
Newmarket.

📷 Nikon D2X, ISO 200, 1/500 at f/5

SOUMILLION CELEBRATES

Christophe Soumillon throws his helmet to
the crowd after Zarkava crowned her unbeaten
career by winning the 2008 Prix de l'Arc de
Triomphe at Longchamp. I have seen thousands
of celebrations but never anything like this.

📷 Nikon D2X, ISO 800, 1/500 at f/5.6

THINKERS AT STRATFORD-UPON-AVON

Two bystanders watch the field stream down the back straight on an autumnal day at Stratford. It was a day of sunshine and showers and the picture was made by the golden glow on the man's coat.

📷 Nikon D2X, ISO 200, 1/640 at f/4

BLACKSMITH HORSESHOE

This is a farrier working on a shoe with a horse at Evan Williams' yard in South Wales.

📷 Nikon D2X, ISO 400, 1/60 at f/2.8

Santa Anita 2008. Olivier Peslier has ridden
the French super filly every time she has run
and he is always hugely appreciative of her. The
clock in the picture shows it was 12–21 pm but
the thermometer was pushing 100 Fahrenheit.
Goldikova was a flyer and she looks it here.

📷 Nikon D3, ISO 200, 1/1000 at f/6.3

FREDDIE HEAD AT LE CYRANO

Deauville, August 2009. Every morning when he is in Deauville Freddie goes here for a coffee and his newspaper. I was sitting further down the cafe and when I spotted him, I crossed the road to shoot this typical French scene using a 70–200mm zoom lens.

Nikon D3, ISO 800, 1/160 at f/5.6

PARIS TURF

Arc weekend at Longchamp, 2009. Goldikova
fever was beginning to build and she was to
win her second Breeders' Cup Mile a month
later. But she actually only finished third in the
soft ground this day at Longchamp. Pictures
sometimes lie.

📷 Nikon D3, ISO 640, 1/500 at f/4

GALLIC EMBRACE

Trainer Freddie Head and jockey Olivier
Peslier celebrate Goldikova's 2009 Breeders'
Cup Mile. It was the second year running they
had triumphed at Santa Anita. Everything was
abuzz but this was a spontaneous moment
of congratulation.

📷 Nikon D3, ISO 400, 1/1250 at f/3.5

TAKE OFF

The final open ditch at Newbury for the
Mandarin Chase in December 2008. Tony
McCoy (far side) and Jimmy McCarthy launch
out against a blue winter sky. To me lift off is
always more exciting than landing.

📷 Nikon D2X, ISO 250, 1/3200 at f/2.8

PRIMARY COLOURS

This is all about colour. It was just an ordinary
juvenile hurdle at Newbury in December 2008
but the simplicity of these primary colours
brightened the winter day.

📷 Nikon D2X, ISO 100, 1/640 at f/5.6

HAYLEY SNOW PRINCESS

Lingfield Park, 30 December 2008. It was an icy cold day but Hayley had just ridden her 100th winner of the year – the first British woman to do this. The coat suits her and matches the snow and enhances a beautiful young face wrapped up in happiness.

📷 Nikon D2X, ISO 100, 1/500 at f/5.6

DOUBLE TAKE

Paul Nicholls and his assistant Dan Skelton use identical gestures at Kempton in February 2009. If you think they look worried, they were. This was in the pre-parade ring before Denman had his first (and unsuccessful) race after his heart problems the previous autumn.

📷 Nikon D2X, ISO 100, 1/500 at f/4

MCCOY BY THE WINDOW

I have taken more photographs of Tony McCoy than anyone, including Frankie Dettori. But in the lead up to Cheltenham 2009 I was trying to find something different to symbolise his lifestyle. This was not set up – I just saw him framed like this looking out from the weighing room at Sandown.

📷 Nikon D3, ISO 200, 1/500 at f/6.3

COLD BREATH

Icy mornings always give the potential of steamy images but what made this picture at Epsom was the zigzag way Jim Boyle's string was coming down the hill. It was as if they were doing it especially to compose a picture.

📷 Nikon D2X, ISO 100, 1/500 at f/6.3

The packed stands and all the different courses that the jockeys need to take during the Festival. The horses are filing out for the four mile amateur riders race in 2009. It gives a sense of the enormity of it all.

📷 Nikon D3, ISO 1600, 1/1250 at f/8

RUBY WALSH CRASHES FROM TATENEN

Third fence, Arkle Trophy, March 2009. Ruby
even falls gracefully. Despite being in the centre
of a big field neither horse nor rider were hurt
and it made a very strong picture. On the first
circuit you can shoot the field head on as they
are going to swing away from you. Normally
you just get colour but this was action too.

📷 Nikon D3, ISO 800, 1/1000 at f/4.5

THE DIGITAL DREAM OF A BOOKIES EYE

Taken from the Desert Orchid stand at the
Cheltenham Festival in March 2009. On a dark
day these new bookmaker pitches really gleam.

📷 Nikon D3, ISO 400, 1/60 at f/10

GODOLPHIN SWIM

Al Quoz Stables, Dubai. The Al Quoz staff
always look immaculate in their Godolphin sky
blue shirts and they give a final symmetry to this
shot. The reins and the walls balance but so do
their shirts and the blue of the water. The horse
seems to be enjoying it too.

📷 Nikon D3, ISO 200, 1/500 at f/9

FOUR WAY FINISH, ASCOT, JULY 2011

The reason this works is the shape of the picture. Symmetry like this is very, very rare. I have been trying to capture this image from the rooftop position for the large handicaps, since the new stand was built in 2006. This was the only time I captured the handicapper's dream finish from there.

📷 Nikon D3, ISO 200, 1/125 at f/13

The Queen smiles at her horse Four Winds
in the pre-parade ring at Newbury. Everyone
knows that the Queen loves racing but this
picture really shows her genuine pleasure in
the horses which she will have known since
they were foals at the royal stud.

📷 Nikon D3, ISO 1000, 1/640 at f/4

PERFECTION TAKES FLIGHT

When Sea The Stars pulled up after winning
the 2000 Guineas in May 2009 we were already
beginning to realise there was something special
about him. Will we ever see better?

📷 Nikon D3, ISO 640, 1/1000 at f/5.6

CLIVE BRITTAIN IN HIS OFFICE

Clive Brittain has had a training licence since 1972. He's in his 70s. The furniture is rather 1970s. He's surrounded by memories of past glories but if you look he's also wearing 'Crocs'.

📷 Nikon D3, ISO 1000, 1/100 at f/3.2

GEORGE BAKER TIMES THREE

I travelled up to Leicester racecourse in 2009 to get this unique photo. The trainer George Baker, holding the horse George Baker, ridden by the jockey George Baker. Harry Findlay had named the horse specifically hoping this treble would come up. Unfortunately the horse didn't.

📷 Nikon D3, ISO 200, 1/400 at f/6.3

THE GORGEOUS KATHERINE JENKINS

At Royal Ascot 2009 the welsh diva made my day. The hat was designed by Philip Tracey, the lady was made in Neath and that's before we come to the voice.

📷 Nikon D3, ISO 100, 1/500 at f/2.8

DENMAN AND KAUTO STAR

June 2009 – these were two Gold Cup winners
on summer holidays. Denman liked to play the
bully but Kauto was always too quick.

Nikon D3, ISO 320, 1/640 at f/4.5

THE FLASH OF HORSES AT CHESTER

By concentrating on the crowd you get this speedy blurred effect on the horses. The shutter is slowed down to 1/40th sec which leaves the foreground and background sharp but leaves you with a sense of the speed at which they are travelling at.

📷 Nikon D3, ISO 100, 1/40 at f/22

Clarefontaine, August 2009. Even in France it is unusual to see such tenderness in public amongst the jockeys. But at Clarefontaine romance seems to hang in the air so why should jockeys not feel it too.

📷 Nikon D3, ISO 200, 1/4000 at f/2.8

DECK CHAIR AT CLAREFONTAINE

Towards the end of the day I saw this lady
sunbathing near the paddock. I was focussed on
her and wanted to see if the jockeys would react
to her and of course they did. It captures the
flowers, the colour, the sensuality of the French.

Nikon D3, ISO 200, 1/3200 at f/3.5

CATCHING THE WORD

A whole battery of voice recorders surround Kieren Fallon at Lingfield after he returned from an 18 month suspension. The camera was on the floor.

📷 Nikon D3, ISO 200, 1/500 at f/9

DEAUVILLE SPLASH

There's a gaucho feel to this. Only two guys but they are handling five horses each. These are polo ponies. We could almost be in Argentina.

📷 Nikon D3, ISO 200, 1/320 at f/8

CHANTAL SUTHERLAND, STAR

Santa Anita, October 2008. We have Hayley Turner but North America has Chantal Sutherland. She has been a top rider in Toronto, Canada, ridden at Breeders' Cups and been voted one of People Magazines '100 Most Beautiful People'. She was standing at 'Clockers Corner' and looked really coolly at the camera.

📷 Nikon D2X, ISO 400, 1/400 at f/2.8

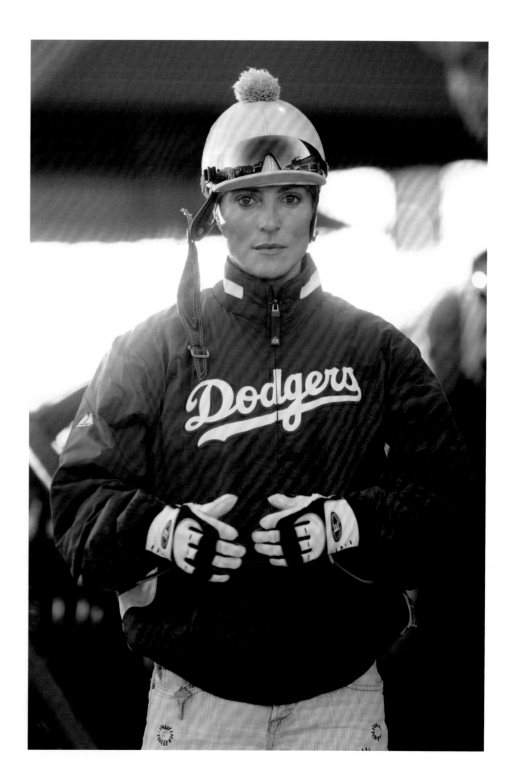

DETTORI FOOTBALL

Frankie battles in the North v South Jockeys
Football match at York in August 2009. We are
so used to seeing him in jockey silks or a flash
suit that it was good to picture him getting
stuck in although he actually lost out here
to the northern jockey Paul Mulrennan.

📷 Nikon D3, ISO 200, 1/500 at f/5

62

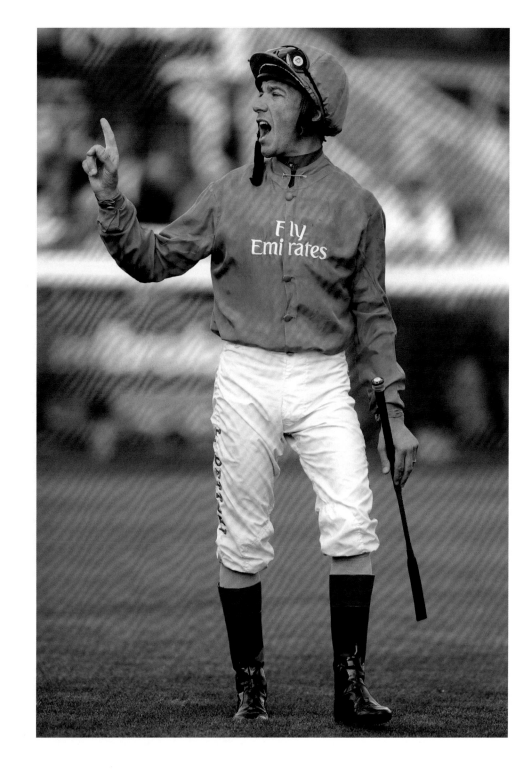

DETTORI NUMBER ONE

Frankie Dettori at Doncaster on the eve of
the 2010 St Leger in which he was to ride the
favourite and subsequently ill-fated Rewilding.
It's a simple image but it shows just how lively
Frankie is – especially when the camera is
on him.

Nikon D3, ISO 200, 1/1000 at f/3.5

THE SEARCH FOR KNOWLEDGE

A punter is hidden behind his *Los Angeles Times* on the morning of Breeders' Cup Day, 2009. Even at this stage there is something slightly desperate about this lonely figure in the never-ending quest for winners.

Nikon D3, ISO 1600, 1/50 at f/4

SEA THE STARS, ARC DE TRIOMPHE, 2009

Out of all the images of Sea The Stars' unique sweep of Group One races that season this is the one that I like best. It has the crowd in the background cheering him on. He and Michael Kinane are a symbol of driving power.

📷 Nikon D3, ISO 640, 1/640 at f/5.6

This was after an early morning gallop for
their Prix de l'Arc de Triomphe hope Conduit
in 2009. Sir Michael Stoute is very animated,
he always uses his hands and body language to
explain things. Ryan is the opposite but is very
confident in his ability.

Nikon D3, ISO 200, 1/500 at f/2.8

OUT OF THE OFFICE

Champion trainer Paul Nicholls looks out of the window of the little office he has above his stable block in Ditcheat, Somerset. Nicholls is a direct man and that comes through in both his look and in the location.

📷 Nikon D3, ISO 1250, 1/320 at f/2.8

Paul Nicholls' stable stars Big Bucks (Rose Luxton), left, and Kauto Star (Donna Blake) swing round the top of his gallop which climbs 232 feet up from the Ditcheat road in just over four furlongs. There's something exciting in the way the gallop clings to the edge of the hill with the spectacular Somerset countryside stretching out below it.

📷 Nikon D3, ISO 320, 1/640 at f/5.6

GARY STEVENS AT SANTA ANITA

Breeders' Cup, November 2009. California
light is fantastic at daybreak. Gary Stevens
was a Breeders' Cup legend as a jockey but he
became even more famous when he starred
in the film *Sea Biscuit*. Yet he belongs to the
mornings. You can see it in his face.

📷 Nikon D3, ISO 200, 1/640 at f/4

Kieren Fallon outside Eddie Delahoussaye's barn at Santa Anita in November 2009. He had been riding for two months after his 18 month drug ban but he was never happier than out here in California.

📷 Nikon D3, ISO 200, 1/160 at f/2.8

BAD HAIR DAY

Pivotal is the Cheveley Park Stud's star stallion at Newmarket. But on this day in November 2009, the wind was doing nothing for his mane. He is an almost ginger chestnut and through the lens he looked a bit like a rock star with a hair dye.

📷 Nikon D3, ISO 1000, 1/500 at f/2.8

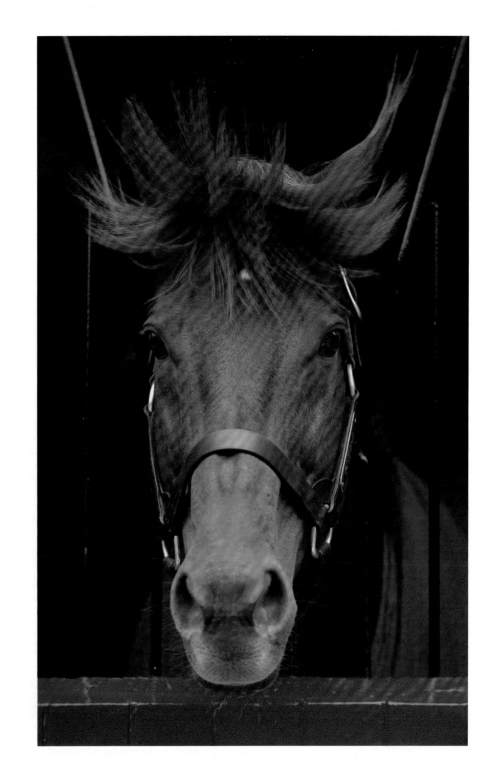

STOUTE IS SATISFIED

Sir Michael Stoute gives me a wink after
Conduit's victory in the Breeders' Cup Turf
at Santa Anita in 2009. He keeps his emotions
in tight before a race but they were really
bubbling out of him here.

📷 Nikon D3, ISO 200, 1/800 at f/4.5

LONELY COWBOY

This is actually Christian Williams leading
a horse at Evan Williams' stable at Llancarfan,
South Wales in December 2009. The rising sun
and the pylons – it could be a cowboy leading
his horse and the way he walks, the streetwise
strut, has a Western feel about it.

📷 Nikon D3, ISO 200, 1/1000 at f/22

PENNY FOR THEM

Sheikh Mohammed looks pensive at the Tattersalls Sales in October 2009. He always dresses informally at the sales but I had not seen him wearing this UAE hat before. It made me realise quite how much responsibility he carries.

📷 Nikon D3, ISO 400, 1/320 at f/4

JIMMY NESBITT, OWNER

He looks as if he is playing the hood but TV star Jimmy Nesbitt was actually reliving the thrill of his horse Riverside Theatre winning at Newbury. It's jockey Barry Geraghty tells the tale.

◻ Nikon D3, ISO 400, 1/500 at f/4.5

JOCKEY CHRISTIAN WILLIAMS IN THE GYM

'Fight Academy Wales', Tenby Green, Near Cardiff, December 2009. The sign outside reads 'Train Hard, Fight Easy'. No jockey I have seen trains harder.

◻ Nikon D3, ISO 4000, 1/200 at f/2.8

ALL WEATHER EARNS ITS NAME

Time was when any fall of snow meant racing
was off. But all weather tracks like this one
at Lingfield give horses – and photographers
– another chance. It's sharp and soft at the
same time.

Nikon D3, ISO 200, 1/1000 at f/5.6

HEAD TO HEAD

Kauto Star and Denman, January 2010. Their showdown in the 2010 Gold Cup was the most hyped race of my time – it was billed as 'The Decider' as each of them had won a Gold Cup already. I wanted to picture them like two heavyweight boxers eyeballing each other at the weigh in. Actually they look quite friendly.

📷 Nikon D3, ISO 400, 1/640 at f/5.6

THE GHOST IN THE SNOW

Snow on the Desert Orchid statue at Kempton
in January 2010. With the light and the snow, it
makes him look like an ice statue. He was one of
my favourite horses. He was much bigger in the
public eye than any other I ever photographed.

📷 Nikon D3, ISO 800, 1/320 at f/2.8

WHERE THE SNOW MEETS THE SKY

Trainer Jim Boyle walks to his string, January
2010. Whenever snow comes I ring Jim at
Epsom and he is unfailingly helpful. The way
he walked towards the gap in the string sets
off the composition here perfectly.

📷 Nikon D3, ISO 200, 1/1000 at f/5.6

SNOW SCENE AT LAMBOURN

January 2010. While I was photographing
Henderson's horses in the snow I suddenly
saw Barry Hills's string walking on the horizon.
The symmetry is perfect.

Nikon D3, ISO 200, 1/1000 at f/4.5

BIRDS EYE VIEW

Goffs Sales Ring, February 2010. All of sales life
is here – the horse in the spotlight, the bidders
by the ring, the gavel and the hands of the
auctioneer.

Nikon D3, ISO 400, 1/80 at f/4

MCCOY AND WALSH IN STEP

The two most famous jump jockeys walking out of the weighing room at Fontwell in January 2010. It was at the time when it was announced that McCoy would ride Denman against Walsh on Kauto Star in the Gold Cup. They are big rivals but the way they are in the picture shows they are great friends too.

📷 Nikon D3, ISO 2000, 1/320 at f/2.8

MCCOY GETS A LIFT

Groundsman Paul Mant gives Tony McCoy a
lift back from the third last hurdle at Fontwell.
I had been there a fortnight before and exactly
the same thing had happened but this time he
was in the McManus yellow and green.

📷 Nikon D3, ISO 1000, 1/1000 at f/4

This was part of a pre-Cheltenham story about Nicky Henderson in March 2010. But what I really like about Lambourn is the way the copses stand out against the sky and the string of horses almost seem to be an extension of it.

📷 Nikon D3, ISO 200, 1/640 at f/7.1

FINISHING TOUCHES AT MEYDAN

The first Dubai World Cup at Meydan was always going to be the most elaborate race day ever staged. From this angle the royal box almost looks like a spaceship and for a few minutes the workers seemed to be having fun.

📷 Nikon D3, ISO 2500, 1/250 at f/3.5

THE ROYAL LOOK

Sheikh Mohammed was the dominant personality on World Cup night. This glimpse through the blur of his entourage shows him with something of a prophet's face.

📷 Nikon D3, ISO 800, 1/2000 at f/2.8

BLANKET FINISH IN DUBAI 2010 WORLD CUP

The winner was the Brazilian-bred, French-trained horse Gloria De Campeao (on the far side) from the South African Lizard's Desire (nearside) and the Dubai-trained Allybar in the centre. It was so close that Kevin Shea on Lizard's Desire thought he had won. The effect is achieved by a slow shutter speed pan.

📷 Nikon D3, ISO 400, 1/60 at f/6.3

MARK JOHNSTON ON THE RUN

When I took this picture of Mark Johnston in April 2010 he had already trained over 100 winners for 16 consecutive seasons. What I liked about the picture is the image of the horses ambling in the background while the trainer is on the run.

Nikon D3, ISO 200, 1/1000 at f/5.6

THAT MCCOY MOMENT

A.P. McCoy wins the Grand National at the fifteenth attempt. How ironic that one of the most driven men in history should win on a horse named Don't Push It. I had photographed all fourteen of his previous Nationals so I knew how much it meant.

Nikon D3, ISO 800, 1/1600 at f/4.5

DRAGON'S BREATH

Trainer Luca Cumani in April 2010. Luca is a smoker but this effect is just from the chill on his breath. I like to shoot portraits into the light against a dark background. The light then defines the silhouette – and in this case gives Luca a smoker's look.

📷 Nikon D3, ISO 400, 1/800 at f/4

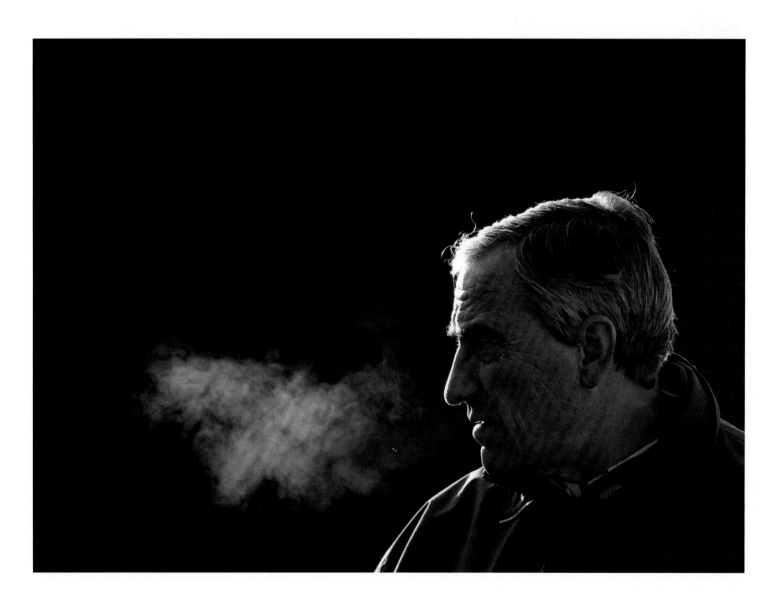

Johnny Murtagh and Aidan O'Brien after the Duke of York Stakes at York in May 2010. It was the last year of their record-breaking partnership and without knowing it, I was picturing the cracks beginning to show. As a photographer I try not to be intrusive but when I see a mood I try to capture it.

Nikon D3, ISO 400, 1/1000 at f/4

TEARS FOR PACO BOY

Richard Hannon is an emotional man. Paco Boy was one of his very best horses but up until the 2010 Lockinge Stakes had always been cast as a seven furlong specialist. This win was redemption time and I got the camera up when the tears rolled down.

📷 Nikon D3, ISO 200, 1/640 at f/4

BIG SKIES AND BLAZING GRASS

Runners break from the stalls on the Rowley
Mile and face seven straining furlongs of
Newmarket turf.

📷 Nikon D3, ISO 400, 1/3200 at f/4.5

FOUR GIRLS AND AN UMBRELLA

Newmarket, May 2010. The glorious British summer won't stop these ladies dressing up in toeless high heels. The joke in the picture is that the umbrella is not from racing but from the Open Championship at Birkdale.

📷 Nikon D3, ISO 400, 1/1000 at f/4.5

DERBY DAY BUSES

Open top buses are part of Derby Day, part of
the tradition of a London day out. This group
are celebrating a winner and to me they look
like a London crowd somehow.

📷 Nikon D3, ISO 200, 1/1000 at f/5.6

**WORKFORCE WINS THE 2010 DERBY
BY SEVEN LENGTHS**

This is taken from a camera which has been clamped to the head on a photographers' stand. It works particularly well because it emphasises the winning margin against the packed stands. It's a good picture.

📷 Nikon D3, ISO 800, 1/4000 at f/5.6

In May 2011 Sir Michael Stoute took Workforce there to see if he could handle something slightly similar to the undulations he would face at Epsom. The horse had worked brilliantly and there is a lot of energy and excitement in the people around him.

📷 Nikon D3, ISO 400, 1/640 at f/4

FRANIE AND THE PAST

Frankie at Sandown in June 2010 sitting in front
of a 19th century painting of the same track 120
years before. Its history is one of racing greatest
strengths and in this picture Frankie shows
that he senses it.

📷 Nikon D3, ISO 1600, 1/160 at f/3.5

FRANKIE AND THE (UNCOMFORTABLE)
PRESENT

An hour after the peace of having his portrait
taken (see opposite) Frankie was reminded of
the risks he takes daily. His horse Toolain had
swerved sharply when in the lead and the jockey
went down amongst the hooves.

Nikon D3, ISO 200, 1/1000 at f/5.6

Royal Ascot hats come in many shapes and fabrics but I had never seen a Faberge-style bird's nest before.

Nikon D3, ISO 200, 1/1600 at f/2.8

100

NEVER MIND A BACK VIEW

There was something elegant about the way Lucinda Hostombe linked arms with her two suitors at Royal Ascot 2010. I also liked the hat!

📷 Nikon D3, ISO 200, 1/500 at f/8

WHO'S A LUCKY BOY THEN?

The great thing about silhouettes is that you can make up your own story to fit the frame. This might just be a guy with his two sisters. On the other hand …

📷 Nikon D3, ISO 200, 1/1000 at f/5.6

Roger Charlton's string at Beckhampton, in
July 2010. What I like about this picture is that
the middle horse has a green cap. It's just one
splash of colour but it makes a nice picture
a special one.

📷 Nikon D3, ISO 200, 1/2000 at f/5.6

EDDERY AND HIS YESTERDAYS

Pat Eddery at his stables near Aylesbury, in 2010,
holds up a picture of himself winning the Arc on
Dancing Brave back in 1986. Training has had its
difficulties for Pat but you can see he is rightly
proud of his past.

📷 Nikon D3, ISO 400, 1/320 at f/5.6

MANY KNAVES ON THE KNAVESMIRE

A huge crowd at York as Wootton Bassett wins
the DBS Premier Yearling Stakes in August
2010. The Ebor Meeting has a flavour of its own
with its special mixture of style and earthiness.
It's both smart and friendly and I wanted to
show how it involves people on both sides
of the track.

📷 Nikon D3, ISO 200, 1/640 at f/7.1

William Buick after winning the 2010 St Leger
on Arctic Cosmos. It was his first classic.
The picture is all about the light, the lovely
white clouds, the blue sky, and the grey and
red braiding of the cap and the comfortable
young man that William has become.

📷 Nikon D3, ISO 400, 1/8000 at f/4

DETTORI FINISH

Goodwood in September 2010. Frankie (near
side) gets Hallberg up to beat Chris Catlin
on Pink Symphony. What I like about the
picture is the perfect distance between the
heads, you can see the horses' eyes clearly, and
the low autumn sun gives a lovely observation
of the shape of the horse's head.

📷 Nikon D3, ISO 200, 1/1000 at f/5.6

HENRY DESK

Sir Henry Cecil sitting in his office at Warren Place. It's all very grand – his tartan curtains, the family tree on the wall, his collection of toy soldiers on the shelves. He is a man at work but he is enjoying being photographed.

📷 Nikon D3, ISO 800, 1/250 at f/2.8

TRUNDLE HILL

Stewards Cup Day at Goodwood in August
2010. There's something very British about this.
The British love camping, barbecues and being
slightly uncomfortable. Up on Trundle Hill they
have an old fashioned betting ring and an ice
cream van but it is a lovely way to spend the day.

📷 Nikon D3, ISO 400, 1/500 at f/13

BREAKFAST WITH DAVID EVANS IN PANDY,
NEAR ABERGAVENNY

David Evans lives in the fast lane but is
unstressed by life. He smokes and drinks at
breakfast but is kind and very comfortable
with himself. I like him a lot. I think this
comes through.

📷 Nikon D3, ISO 1250, 1/160 at f/2.8

MAN IN THE SHADOWS

Dave Roberts is the jockeys' agent who has
helped Tony McCoy break all these records.
He is an unknown character who lives in this
Victorian house in Redhill and so I wanted to
picture him as a man who plays in the shadows.
There's a touch of the Marlon Brando character
Kurtz in *Apocalypse Now*.

📷 Nikon D3, ISO 400, 1/1000 at f/3.5

THUMBS UP FROM PAUL HANAGAN

Paul Hanagan is happy after winning his first Group One race with Wootton Bassett in the Prix Jean Luc Lagardere (Grand Criterium) at Longchamp on Arc day 2010. Paul was the star of that autumn and his enjoyment of his run towards his first jockeys' championship really showed.

📷 Nikon D3, ISO 400, 1/500 at f/4.5

JOHN MAGNIER SOLO

The Coolmore boss has a rare moment alone at Book One of the premier Tattersalls Yearling Sales. John normally has all his team around him but just for once he was standing on his own in the bidding area. It wasn't something I should miss.

📷 Nikon D3, ISO 2500, 1/500 at f/2.8

RYAN'S SMILE

Ryan Moore after winning the Arc de
Triomphe on Workforce in 2010. Ryan rarely
smiles, even in victory, but here, cantering back
with the winner's rug, I could really picture
his sense of achievement – and what a ride
he had given Workforce.

📷 Nikon D3, ISO 400, 1/1000 at f/5

PHILIP HOBBS' STRING ONE EARLY MORNING

This was pre Cheltenham 2011 and I loved the glow of promise that came from the sun on the mist that comes up from the Bristol Channel.

📷 Nikon D3, ISO 200, 1/500 at f/4

THE HANDS OF THE HEALER

Trainer Henry Cecil cups his hands up to
Twice Over after that colt has won his second
Champion Stakes in 2010. Henry cuts an elegant
figure but when he puts his hands to a horse you
can see a real tenderness there.

📷 Nikon D3, ISO 1000, 1/500 at f/4.5

HARBINGER HEAVEN

Jockey Olivier Peslier reaches forward in
congratulation as Harbinger slaughters his King
George VI and Queen Elisabeth II Stakes rivals,
including Derby winner Workforce. It wasn't
a win, it was a rout.

📷 Nikon D3, ISO 400, 1/2000 at f/2.8

LONE HORSE ON THE SKYLINE

A single horse gallop up Fishers Hill near Upper Lambourn in October 2010. This is one of my favourite pictures because of its simplicity. You know it's a racehorse because of the running rails. You can see the speed from the rider's body position. And you appreciate it's autumn from the sharp orange glow.

📷 Nikon D3, ISO 800, 1/800 at f/2.8

ZENYATTA'S HORSE BOX

America loves to have things big and loud. So,
to carry Zenyatta, the horse transporter had to
be as brash, muscled and polished as this one.
And we haven't even shown you the police cars.

📷 Nikon D3, ISO 400, 1/1000 at f/8

FLYING FRANKIE

Frankie Dettori after winning the Breeders'
Cup Turf on Dangerous Midge in 2010. Frankie
is a showman. Breeders' Cup Day is the biggest
show in the game. I particularly like this because
the unsaddling enclosure was in deep shade so
I had a go with my flash to see if I could light
him against it. He jumped extra high and it
worked perfectly.

📷 Nikon D3, ISO 1600, 1/1600 at f/2.8

SUNSET FOR ZENYATTA

This was my first look at the floodlights at
Churchill Downs and they provided a dramatic
backstop for the most dramatic of finishes –
Zenyatta just failing to nail Blame and take
her unbeaten run to 20.

📷 Nikon D3, ISO 2500, 1/1600 at f/2.8

REACHING FOR THE LAST DITCH

Ascot, November 2010. Barry Geraghty
on Master Of The Hall (far side) and Tom
Scudamore on Fredo at full stretch. Master
Of The Hall was the winner but I love the
completely committed power of both of them.

📷 Nikon D3, ISO 400, 1/3200 at f/4.5

Another view of the famous finish of the 2010
Breeders' Cup Classic as Blame (right) just holds
off Zenyatta. They are caught in the strip light
of the finishing line. Dirt is flying, it covers
both horses, they are both at maximum power
and I like the way the tungsten light exaggerates
the colours against the darkness.

📷 Nikon D3, ISO 2500, 1/1250 at f/4

A SAD ENDING TO A GREAT RACE

Even though Blame was the winner of the 2010 Breeders' Cup Classic, the story was of Zenyatta's defeat coming from what was an impossible position so far back. The expression on jockey Mike Smith's face says it all as he comes back to unsaddle and the dirt-plastered mare seems fed up too.

📷 Nikon D3, ISO 3200, 1/250 at f/2.8

WINTER SLOG

Towcester, December 2010. One of the hardest
pictures to get is horses racing in the snow. It
was forecast that morning but it was the last race
and nearly dark before the snow finally came.

📷 Nikon D3, ISO 4000, 1/200 at f/4

RACING TO GO AHEAD — YES OR NO?

Clerk of the course Andrew Cooper at
Sandown. A covering of snow makes a mundane
background look totally different and I love the
contrast between Andrew, the fences and the
half furlong marker.

📷 Nikon D3, ISO 640, 1/640 at f/7.1

SNOW AND THE AMATEURS

The riders for an amateur race at Folkestone
walk out into a snowstorm. It's unusual because
if it is snowing as hard as this racing has
usually been abandoned. Mind you it was soon
afterwards and the race never happened.

📷 Nikon D3, ISO 640, 1/500 at f/5.6

RICHARD JOHNSON AMIDST THE GREYS

Richard is a tremendous jockey and is just
so unlucky to be the perpetual runner up to
McCoy. I was doing a feature on him in March
2011 and even though you can only see his face,
the focus draws you in.

📷 Nikon D3, ISO 500, 1/1000 at f/2.8

ICEBOX KEMPTON UNDER THE LIGHTS

The cold spell in December 2010 had gone on
for weeks. This was the last race of the day and
the floodlights on the horses emphasise the
gloom and the cold in the background.

📷 Nikon D3, ISO 400, 1/500 at f/2.8

CHASING THE LIGHT

Chasers at Plumpton, 2 January 2011. At this
time of year, you want to use whatever light is
available to give a contrast. At Plumpton there
is this very pleasing tree at the top of the hill on
the chase course. I wanted to picture it in profile
and hope that the horses would create this sense
of pursuit for me.

📷 Nikon D3, ISO 200, 1/4000 at f/4.5

LONG RUN TAKES KAUTO STAR

King George VI Chase, Kempton, 2010.
The reason I like this picture is the unusual
slant of the horse's stride. They are crossing
the all weather surface as they take the tight
turn after the winning post. I have never seen
a cornering balance like this.

📷 Nikon D3, ISO 2500, 1/1000 at f/4

ALLO ALLO

An archetypal punter struggles with the form
in Paris on Arc weekend in 2010. They did not
have the *Racing Post* in 'Allo Allo' days but this
guy looked too like the Rene Artois character
for me to miss.

📷 Nikon D3, ISO 400, 1/1250 at f/2.8

FFOS LAS FROM THE AIR

This is taken from the helicopter of Dai Walters, owner of Ffos Las. I was much influenced by aerial shots in the David Attenborough series 'Planet Earth' in which the camels show shadows across the sand. Here it works equally well for horses on grass.

📷 Nikon D3, ISO 400, 1/1000 at f/5.6

Champion Hurdle favourite Binocular
works at Seven Barrows, near Lambourn,
in November 2010. The key to this picture is
the watching figure of Henderson's long serving
head man Corky Browne. The boss was away
but Corky was there as he has been from the
very beginning.

Nikon D3, ISO 400, 1/2000 at f/5

Cheltenham, St Patrick's Day, 2011. The Irish had swept the board the previous day and everything green seemed to be celebrating. Of course this was a bit of a corny stunt but these were a pretty athletic pair of Leprechauns who leapt in perfect tandem to create this image.

📷 Nikon D3, ISO 200, 1/2000 at f/4

FACE OF A CHAMPION

Ruby Walsh at Sandown the weekend before the
2011 Cheltenham Festival. Ruby had taken such
a heavy fall in Ireland earlier in the week that
many thought he would miss Cheltenham. He
rode at Sandown to prove otherwise. See it in
his face. He ended up top jockey once again.

📷 Nikon D3, ISO 400, 1/2500 at f/4

Trainer Nicky Henderson with brothers
Sam (right) and Marcus Waley Cohen on
the winners' rostrum after Long Run had
won the 2011 Cheltenham Gold Cup.

📷 Nikon D3, ISO 640, 1/800 at f/4

A BIG FIELD FOR THE COUNTY HURDLE

Cheltenham. March 2011. On the last day the
final hurdle was moved a long way forward.
This meant you could put a camera as close as
you dared. This ensured a tremendous amount
of action in the picture.

📷 Nikon D3, ISO 400, 1/4000 at f/4

Jonjo O'Neill comes down the Aintree steps in the colours of his patron JP McManus before the 2011 charity race. It was 25 years since he retired as a jockey and he was loving it. And they were loving him. They always did.

Nikon D3, ISO 400, 1/640 at f/5

DONALD MCCAIN AND BALLABRIGGS

This was a week before Ballabriggs won the
2011 Grand National. Trainer and horse are in
a standard pose but there is something pleasing
in the movement of Ballabriggs and the ease in
Donald's features. Did he know something?

📷 Nikon D3, ISO 200, 1/1000 at f/5.6

SHEIKH AND AIDAN

This was Aidan O'Brien's first visit to Meydan, in March 2011. Sheikh Mohammed in his traditional robes is the symbol of welcome.

📷 Nikon D3, ISO 200, 1/80 at f/4

AL QUOZ AND DUBAI CITYSCAPE

Al Quoz is Sheikh Mohammed's own racing stables. Everything is immaculate, the grass perfect and I wanted to link the horse and the palm trees with Dubai city in the background, including the Burj Khalifa, the world's tallest building.

📷 Nikon D3, ISO 200, 1/640 at f/6.3

For me the Grand National has four potential
images, the start, the water, the Chair and
the finish. Uniquely this year, the winner was
already clear with a whole circuit to go.

📷 Nikon D3, ISO 640, 1/3200 at f/5

WHERE DID YOU GET THOSE COLOURS?

Frankie Dettori has a quizzical look at Mickael Barzalona, the young French jockey who is a prospective superstar of the future.

📷 Nikon D3, ISO 1250, 1/1000 at f/4

The Derby, 2011. The Queen had the favourite Carlton House but this picture is taken after he had only finished third and she is looking down from the Royal Box. She is flanked by Lord Vestey, Prince Edward and Sir Michael Oswald. As you can see, the race must have mattered to the Queen.

📷 Nikon D3, ISO 400, 1/1000 at f/4.5

THE BANKS AT PUNCHESTOWN

Runners jumping fence 14 'The Old Double'
at Punchestown in May 2011. This is one of the
most difficult obstacles I have ever pictured. By
positioning a camera with 14mm lens on top of
the bank I could get the effect of take-off and
landing in one.

📷 Nikon D3, ISO 400, 1/2500 at f/4

Canford Cliffs has just trounced the brilliant
French mare Goldikova in the Queen Anne
Stakes, the very first race of Royal Ascot 2011.
In the winners' enclosure I am looking for
emotion – and here we got it.

📷 Nikon D3, ISO 200, 1/1000 at f/5.6

LESTER PIGGOTT, MAY 2011

Lester was born in 1935 but he was still loose
and flexible when I asked him to sit in his
garden. He's still a legend and it was good for
me and the picture to have him on his own.

📷 Nikon D3, ISO 200, 1/400 at f/2

This is just after the Queen's unveiling of the bronze statue of the record breaking, four time Gold Cup winner Yeats on the opening day of Royal Ascot 2011. John Magnier has wandered off from the official party to get close to the horse who made history for him.

📷 Nikon D3, ISO 200, 1/640 at f/5.6

TAXI RIDE

The 18-year-old Adrian Heskin had a painful introduction to the Aintree fences in April 2011 but this London-style black cab came to his rescue. Actually it was the one I and *Guardian* photographer Tom Jenkins had hired for the day.

📷 Nikon D3, ISO 400, 1/1250 at f/4

THE DUEL ON THE DOWNS

Frankel and Canford Cliffs at the end of the 2011 Sussex Stakes at Goodwood. Using the remote camera from the ground not only grabs the image of Frankel in full flight but shows just how far Canford Cliffs had drifted under pressure in what was to be his last ever race.

📷 Nikon D3, ISO 1000, 1/4000 at f/3.5

THE LEGEND THAT WAS FRANKEL

The horse Frankel was named after the late, great Bobby Frankel pictured here with his horses before the 2008 Breeders' Cup a year before he died. It was the last picture I took of him.

📷 Nikon D2X, ISO 400, 1/250 at f/8

FRANKEL SUPERSTAR

The race may have been more of a struggle than expected but afterwards everyone wanted a piece of him. With his ears pricked and his jockey congratulating him, he posed here as a victor should.

📷 Nikon D3, ISO 200, 1/1000 at f/5.6

EIGHT SETS OF LEGS

Royal Ascot 2011. The picture works because the ladies are all nicely spaced out and if you think that some of the legs are crossed a bit tightly you are probably right. For they were sitting outside the ladies loo.

Nikon D3, ISO 400, 1/800 at f/4.5

AN OBE FOR AP

Dr Anthony McCoy (honorary doctorate from
Belfast University) holds up his latest honour
in the courtyard of Buckingham Palace in June
2011. I have taken so many pictures of AP that
this time I focussed on the medal – if you look
very closely you can see it says: 'For God and
the Empire'.

📷 Nikon D3, ISO 400, 1/500 at f/6.3

HOPE LIVES IN PINK

A wet scene on Ladies Day at Royal Ascot 2011.
Pictures do not need to be complicated. This
lady is the focus of the picture but everything
compliments her from the pink bench beside
her to the regularity of the line opposite.

📷 Nikon D3, ISO 800, 1/1000 at f/4

MASSED RANKS ON WARREN HILL

April is the busiest and most hopeful month at Newmarket. With the mist, the picture had plenty of mystery and possibility about it.

📷 Nikon D3, ISO 200, 1/500 at f/8

ACKNOWLEDGEMENTS

I should like to thank my family, all my many friends and, in particular, *Racing Post* colleagues who have been so generous with their time and help in the preparation of this book.

My undying thanks go to Jilly Cooper for her flatteringly kind words in the foreword to *Beyond The Frame*.

Naturally, I thank the publishers for their tireless support and encouragement while the designer, Rachel Bray, has been inspirational. Others who have helped so much include wise Jim Tierney, Geoffrey Hughes at the Osborne Studio Gallery, Alan Byrne, the CEO of the *Racing Post*, legendary writer Brough Scott, and that supreme sports photographer Chris Smith. All have displayed great humour and patience in their dealings with me.